Facts About the Red Wolf

By Lisa Strattin

© 2020 Lisa Strattin

FREE BOOK

FREE FOR ALL SUBSCRIBERS

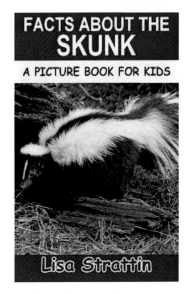

LisaStrattin.com/Subscribe-Here

BOX SET

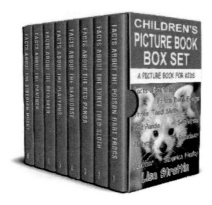

- FACTS ABOUT THE POISON DART FROGS
- FACTS ABOUT THE THREE TOED SLOTH
- FACTS ABOUT THE RED PANDA
- FACTS ABOUT THE SEAHORSE
- FACTS ABOUT THE PLATYPUS
- FACTS ABOUT THE REINDEER
- FACTS ABOUT THE PANTHER
- FACTS ABOUT THE SIBERIAN HUSKY

LisaStrattin.com/BookBundle

Facts for Kids Picture Books by Lisa Strattin

Little Blue Penguin, Vol 92

Chipmunk, Vol 5

Frilled Lizard, Vol 39

Blue and Gold Macaw, Vol 13

Poison Dart Frogs, Vol 50

Blue Tarantula, Vol 115

African Elephants, Vol 8

Amur Leopard, Vol 89

Sabre Tooth Tiger, Vol 167

Baboon, Vol 174

Sign Up for New Release Emails Here

LisaStrattin.com/subscribe-here

COVER IMAGE

https://www.flickr.com/photos/usfwssoutheast/40907778685/

ADDITIONAL IMAGES

https://www.flickr.com/photos/7326810@N08/4108641262

https://www.flickr.com/photos/47847725@N04/4530702213/

https://www.flickr.com/photos/tmwolf/3225287939/

https://www.flickr.com/photos/37467370@N08/16010905248/

https://www.flickr.com/photos/7326810@N08/4093910057

https://www.flickr.com/photos/trackthepack/6189225921/

https://www.flickr.com/photos/trackthepack/7747777230/

https://www.flickr.com/photos/trackthepack/6350801869/

https://www.flickr.com/photos/7326810@N08/4108641976

https://www.flickr.com/photos/lblkytn/8742251484/

Contents

INTRODUCTION

The Red Wolf lives in the marshes of southern regions of Eastern North America. They are a medium-sized wolf.

CHARACTERISTICS

The Red Wolf is usually smaller than the Grey Wolf. They are named because of the cinnamon color of their fur. They are social and live within a group of other Red Wolves. The group is called a "pack." In each pack of up to 10 animals, there is one dominant male and female plus their young.

They are extremely territorial and will fiercely protect their home range area from intruders.

APPEARANCE

Besides the brownish-red cinnamon colored fur, the Red Wolves have dark patches of fur on their back. They also have wide noses and ears that seem to be too big for their head.

REPRODUCTION

At about 2 years of age, the female Red Wolf can have babies. They usually mate in the Spring months of February through March. In one litter, after a 2 month pregnancy, the mother can have as many as 10 babies, which are called "cubs."

The cubs are looked after by all the animals in the pack until they are able to go out and hunt for their own food. Then they might stay with their parents or go off on their own to start their own family and pack.

LIFE SPAN

On average, a Red Wolf will live for 10 to 12 years or so.

SIZE

An adult Red Wolf can weigh up to 90 pounds and grow to be almost 4 feet long!

HABITAT

The Red Wolf is native to several regions of the United States and can be seen in the South all the way from Texas to Florida. They have also been known to live further up the East Coast all the way to New York. They prefer forested areas, prairie areas on the coasts, or swamplands. In these areas, the Red Wolf has been able to be dominant as a top predator. Now, they are located mainly in a legally protected area of North Carolina.

DIET

Red Wolves eat a lot of small animals that live on the ground. Their main diet includes: rodents, rats, birds, and raccoons. But, they will occasionally go after a large animal, like a deer, when they go hunting as a pack. When hunting as a pack, they work together to surround and corner the animal they want to catch.

ENEMIES

In their native habitat, there are not many predators of the Red Wolf. A Coyote or the larger Grey Wolf will hunt and kill them, but most animals where they live are prey to the Red Wolf, instead of a threat.

SUITABILITY AS PETS

A Red Wolf is not really suitable to be a pet. They are wild animals and like to catch and kill their own food, so it would be difficult to provide a proper habitat for one in your back yard. They are strong and territorial, so it would be hard to share their space with them.

You might be able to see them at your local zoo. If they have built an appropriate place for them to live, you can go there to watch and learn about them.

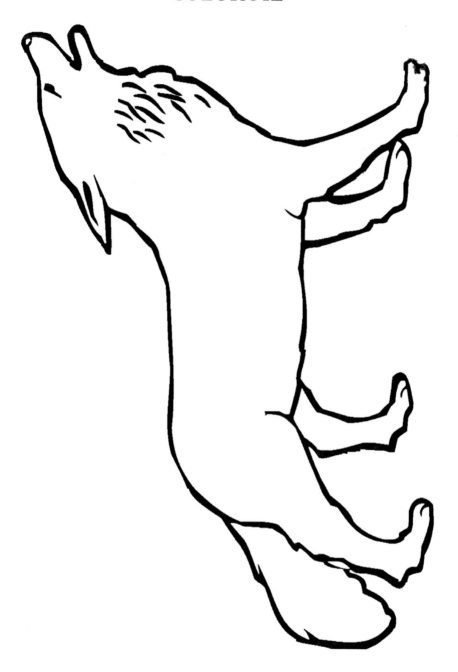

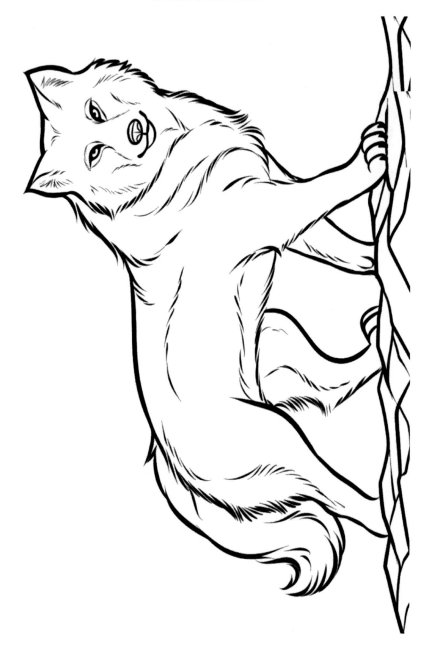

COLOR ME

COLOR ME

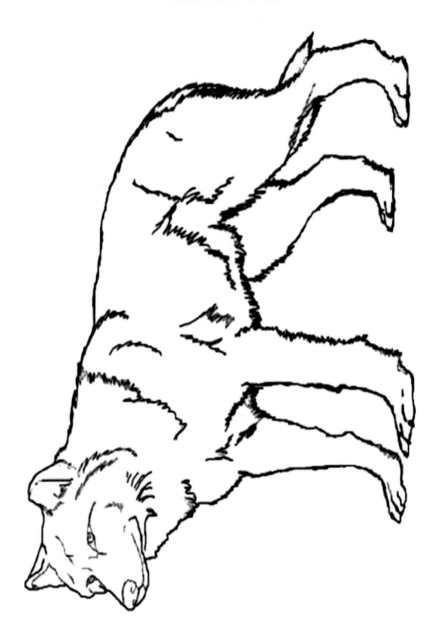

COLOR ME

COLOR ME

COLOR ME

Please leave me a review here:

LisaStrattin.com/Review-Vol-365

For more Kindle Downloads Visit Lisa Strattin
Author Page on Amazon Author Central

amazon.com/author/lisastrattin

To see upcoming titles, visit my website at
LisaStrattin.com– most books available on Kindle!

LisaStrattin.com

FREE BOOK

FOR ALL SUBSCRIBERS – SIGN UP NOW

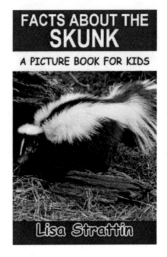

LisaStrattin.com/Subscribe-Here

LisaStrattin.com/Facebook

LisaStrattin.com/Youtube

Made in United States
North Haven, CT
14 September 2022

24121032R20024